GOD HAS NOT GIVEN US THE SPIRIT OF FEAR: BUT OF
POWER, AND OF LOVE, AND A SOUND MIND

II TIMOTHY 1:7

NO FEAR:
THE LORD'S REDEMPTION

Jones Publishing LLC

First Edition 2011
Cover Design by Elizabeth E Rios-Jones
Library of Congress Data
Jones, Elton D.
No Fear: The Lord's Redemption / Elton D. Jones
p. cm.
ISBN 978-0-9836783-1-1 pbk.
PCN
1.Inspirational & Religious-Poetry.
2. African Americans-Poetry.

~ Acknowledgement ~

THIS BOOK I DEDICATE TO MY LORD GOD AND SAVIOR,
JESUS CHRIST.
THANK YOU GOD, FOR SAVING A WRETCH LIKE ME.
I WILL PRAISE AND GLORIFY YOUR NAME CONTINUALLY.
TO THE MEMBERS
OF FEARLESS FAITH CHURCH; THANK YOU ALL FOR BELIEVING
AND MOTIVATING ME TO DO BETTER IN THE NAME OF THE LORD.
BLESS YOU PASTOR COTTON! YOU ARE MY HERO.
THANK YOU FOR ALL OF THE KIND WORDS AND
ENCOURAGEMENT.
YOUR BELIEF IS CONTAGIOUS!

CONTENTS

IT IS FOR THIS REASON THAT I HAVE SAVED YOUR LIFE. SO THAT I MAY SHOW MY POWER IN YOU. AND THAT MY NAME SHALL BE DECLARED THROUGHOUT ALL OF THE EARTH.

EXODUS 9:16

FOR I AM THE LORD YOUR GOD. YOU SHALL THEREFORE CONSECRATE YOURSELVES, AND YOU SHALL BE HOLY; FOR I AM HOLY. NEITHER SHALL YOU DEFILE YOURSELVES WITH ANY CREEPING THING THAT CREEPS ON THE EARTH.

LEVITICUS 11:44

THEN I WILL CONFESS TO YOU THAT YOUR OWN RIGHT HAND CAN SAVE YOU.

JOB 40:14

WITH MEN IT IS IMPOSSIBLE, BUT NOT WITH GOD; FOR
WITH GOD ALL THINGS ARE POSSIBLE.

MARK 10:27

MY GRACE IS SUFFICIENT FOR YOU, FOR MY STRENGTH IS
MADE PERFECT IN WEAKNESS.

2 CORINTHIANS 12:9

IT IS FOR THIS REASON THAT I HAVE SAVED YOUR LIFE. SO THAT I MAY SHOW MY POWER IN YOU. AND THAT MY NAME SHALL BE DECLARED THROUGHOUT ALL OF THE EARTH.

EXODUS 9:16

COME HUNGRY; LEAVE HAPPY

We are but spiritual babes, still suckling on milk.
We should be ready for solid foods but,
Understanding only comes by the reading of It.
Have you ever heard what David ate? When he and his
Men could find none other to eat?
Coming out of a spiritual fast, feeling nutrition depleted.
My Father wasn't even mad!
Just one more instance for Jesus to use in a parable for
Teaching us.
Leavened or unleavened? Our bread no longer depends
On the time of the year.
We live in these times of abundance!
Leavened bread fills our bodies in all times throughout the years.
Man cannot live by bread alone!
So we devour this word like it's a New Years Day lock-in,
Knowing that this will keep our souls close to His.
There's something going on outside,
And it's bigger than any of us may think.
Take advantage of this day Saints:
Stay and eat!
Bonded in fellowship with those
We love.
Now needing to know more about those we already love.
Without the power of the Lord, where would we be?

Never woulda made it!

No.....no...I never coulda made it!

Wouldn't be so grateful for this food you gave us.

satan wants to tempt us

Telling us to turn this stone into bread!

I'll never eat food again before I walk the path

he's led.

Envisioned a plan in his head,

All with the attempt to capture us.

Stand behind us satan!

It's our Lord thy God who continues to lead us in this path we on.

Being that She feeds the sparrows and squirrels......

How will She not feed Her young boys and girls?

Harmonious by nature so we sing Psalms together while we eat.

Together holding hands in prayer

Directed up in all faith to the King.

In here we know that all is O.K.!

Out there the world is gone crazy.

Trying to attack us!

We welcome you to Our Father's house:

Still in here you try and attack us!

Hallowed beThy name.

In Our Father's house there's no need for light;

His love continually reigns, shining down the brightest of light.

Shining down upon us

Even in our darkest of days.

Only God can cause this type of explosion
And it only sparks according to our faith.
Igniting our ignitions!
So we thank you for coming for this fuel,
And we pray that you will receive
A spiritual breakthrough.
Compliments to the chefs,
And to those who provided the produce.
If you got the time,
Stay around and help us clean this mess!
If that's what the Holy Spirit so informs you to do.

EVERYTHING COMES WITH A PRICE

Money, fame, or massive success.

What's the price we must pay in order to be our absolute best?

Money won't pay my way out of this,

How many lives must be lost in this mess?

Just to move one more step........

What is it that I must be willing to give up?

House? Daughter? Son? Wife and cars?

Many of us must even spend some time behind bars.

Dead to this world, until we are alive in the King.

Many people will even sell their own souls

To acquire the things that bling!

Even love acquired, in this world ain't free.

Lost so much of my own world

That I know the King now lives through me.

All things in the world

Come to those who believe.

But what exactly is it that I'm believing in?

Those things that are seen?

Or those unseen?

What are you willing to pay

If one could answer all of your wildest dreams?

Make all of your goals and dreams come to life.

What would you be willing to pay as the price?

Kids? Time? Or maybe even your very own life?

What are you willing to pay?

If I promised to make all of your hurt go away?

No more pain, sin or fear of death.

Until there is none of me left!

I die everyday!.

Just a ghostly aspiration,

Wanting to ascend to the King.

What is the price we must pay,

In order to sit to the left and the right of our King?

This being ain't even enough

The flesh and blood will only fade away.

Call we 007

Because we have to die another day.

How much is in your jackpot?

And to He what is it worth?

Thank you for the cursing on man of death

And for women to conceive for childbirth.

A blessing from a cursing is what

We are promised by Zechariah 8: 13.

Give me no credit for any of this,

These words are all derived by a higher being.

A blueprint from the King

All exposed in The Book.

Imprinted in our hearts with Love

We could never thank you enough.

For your word allows a fresh start to each of us:
With alcohol and drugs am I willing to part?
When your voice advises me that it's time for a change of heart.
What's the jump start
2 rekindle my cold heart?
Will cheerfully give it all away
But from your word Lord,
We will never stay apart.

DEAR MINISTER BRISCOE

I hope you don't mind,
But all week your sermon has been rumbling through my mind,
Not easily broken!
Three words you left in our mindz.
I went through the bible looking,
To perform a quick sweep
Of circumstances and people who are not broken with ease:
The agreement with Abraham and his descendants;
The promise of Isaac to be born from Sarah;
Jacob wrestles with The Word, until his hip is dislocated;
Joseph is sold into slavery after sharing his dream,
And before becoming ruler over all of Egypt;
Moses and Aaron are Gods chosen,
In a land riddled with unbelievers;
Yet and still, Leviticus 26:40 reminds us of Gods saying:
FOR THEIR GOOD, I WILL REMEMBER THEIR ANCESTOR'S
AGREEMENT!
Through it all, we must always keep believing.
In Numbers 34, the Lord says to Moses:
GIVE THIS COMMAND TO THE PEOPLE OF ISRAEL,
YOU WILL SOON ENTER CANAAN AND IT WILL BE YOURS;
In Deuteronomy the promise to Abraham is fulfilled to man
And Moses appoints 12 leaders over the many nations;
Re-read Deuteronomy 4:32 if you need more confirmation.

The Lord is our great redeemer,

Through whatever we may be facing!

The Lord spoke from the fire on Mt. Sinai to make

The agreement with Israel;

Deuteronomy 7 tells us of a chosen generation;

Much happens in Deuteronomy yet how many of us can

Sing the Song of Moses?

Do you know what happens

After the people are blessed by Moses?

Although Moses couldn't make it,

It is Joshua who welcomes the people;

Rahab hid the spies and God spared her life

Along with all those who were dwelling inside;

The priest had to step their feet into the water of the Jordan

Before the flowing would cease,

Allowing the people and Joshua to pass through with ease;

Have you reminisced of the 12 rocks left behind

To remind us of this historic passage through time?

Read in Judges of the power of Sampson,

And all of the trials and tribulations he had to fight;

Ask Ruth about the importance of connecting with family;

Turn to 1 Samuel and speak with Hannah

About the significance of giving thanks to our Lord!

How'd David overcome Goliath with no sword?

Find 2 Samuel 7:18 to see David become King

And pray to the God of his living being;

Take notice of Elijah as the whirlwind ascends him to heaven;
If the widow never would have asked Elisha for help
How would the empty jars ever be filled with oil?
The Shulamite woman became pregnant
After trusting Elisha to live in her home;
Rather than to plead for riches,
Solomon asks for wisdom and understanding to discern justice;
Look to Ezra to know the importance to our God
Of finding ITS lost things;
Re-research in 2 Nehemiah 9:5 and seek the people's prayers;
What do you know about the people's agreement?
The move into Jerusalem?
How is it that Esther manages to save her people?
If Job is a man of God
Why is it that he suffers so?
How many Psalms could you recite
If I first took away your Bible and notes?
When exactly have we become a kin to Wisdom, and
Understanding our next of kin,
Why don't you open up the book of Proverbs
To see how it all fits in?
Where's the conundrum in Ecclesiastes? Is it in
The beauty of the Song of Solomon?
A love song like Prufrock
Onto the troubled Isaiah.
We're still trying to understand Jeremiah's message...

12

Why would Jerusalem have so many Lamentations
When She is the Chosen City?
Does reading the book of Ezekiel make me a
Visionary or a dreamer?
Is Daniel our true visionary?
Of the King's dreams he found the meaning;
Can you see the face of King Nebuchadnezzar
When he looked into the furnace to find one more than
The initial three!
Uncharred, unburned, unbound, and stepping out of the fire with
Ease;
How will we look into souls to become like Hosea?
Living in order to suffer
And continuing to find only joy and good Measure.
What will we learn by studying Joel, Amos or Obadiah?
Jonah illustrates a game of hide and seek
That we all at one time or another play.
Pretending that we can duck and dodge from He
As if He doesn't know the way we taking.
Micah stood up as a friend for God till his last day;
Nahum, Habakkuk, Zephaniah;
Why should I keep reading this?
The book of Haggai eventually rebuilds the temple;
Zechariah encourages the people;
Malachi announces the end to the Old Testament
While proclaiming of the new.

Which book should we be studying in?

Do we just focus forward to the Revelation?

How do we first learn to play a board game that's new?

The instructions not only show all the pieces involved in the Game's Play,

But the step by step construction of the board.

Next, a play by play is given of how and when

The game will be no more!

I need to know more.

Now it's the New Testament I'm chasing Him in.

Reading of the gang of misfits Jesus labeled friends of His

So God allowed them to do great things for Him.

How about you take your own journey through The Revelation

And I'll do the same thing.

Then come back and we'll talk about our findings.

And look to see the meanings.

No, we're not easily broken

Although our imperfections flow through!

He placed us here to allow his glory to continue flowing

Through me and through you.

IN HIS PRESENCE

Keeping us safe through these dark nights.

When we thought that all the walls were caved in,

Ceiling destroyed.

As if a natural disaster had finally

Come to an abrupt end.

No need to look around, Jesus is this whirlwind of peace.

Even when it is that we stop, the Spirit keeps moving right on

Through me.

No matter how much the world tries to stop us!

Give us peace.

The ability to be still and just listen to our heart beat!

Misguided by our looks into the world;

The misrepresentation that we can sometime see.

When the whole time we are nestled in your heart.

You are the sunshine that we need!

Here within your Love is where we long to be.

So many say that they can't feel you

But we know that you shine down upon us

Radiating all of the positive heat that you bring.

Warming our soul with your innate goodness!

If you tell me to,

I'll give this seat away

So that others may too reach your fullness!

Full of your capacity, is where we will remain.

With the power that you give to us

We are able to maintain.
The life of me is dead
It is you that now leads the way.
Illuminating our world
As we learn to tap into your spiritual way.
Spiritual goodness is what you give to us
When within the walls of your Kingdom we remain.
We know that you are here with us
Although physically we can't see your shell.
Living in this pleasure seeking generation
We don't even yearn to see you.
Just keep on trusting and believing in YOU
Knowing that your word already tells us that you're there.
This world tells us that we're crazy,
And a bit weird,
But we don't even care.
Not even Jesus was accepted
Though he gave Himself to show God's Love is everywhere.
We sit here lost in your presence;
Following you wherever it is that you may go.
Like a lost puppy,
We stare to you as our master,
Waiting for you to tell us which Way to go.
Through the cold or the heat
It doesn't even matter.

Knowing that you'll show us the correct way;
The way out of this natural disaster.
This horrendous situation has to eventually end.
Your word tells us the truth
And in it we will always live.
You are our living God
It is by your presence that we will always forgive.
Thank you Lord Jesus,
For placing your stamp across our face.
Without your Son, how is it that we would ever be
Going in the correct way?
No fire to light this dark world up.
A cold Michigan night needs Heat!
Can you imagine cooking a recipe
Without the seasoning?
Dry, would our wells be
Now where is it that our buckets may drink?
Unbounded to a connection
So where does the multiplication begin?
I'm good with numbers
And the most important number for us is Won.
Mystically an aggregate of three:
The Father, The Son, and the Holy Spirit!
All here near to us.
In Her presence,
Is where I long to live.

18

FOR I AM THE LORD YOUR GOD. YOU SHALL THEREFORE
CONSECRATE YOURSELVES, AND YOU SHALL BE HOLY; FOR
I AM HOLY. NEITHER SHALL YOU DEFILE YOURSELVES
WITH ANY MANNER OF CREEPING THING THAT CREEPS
ON THE EARTH.

LEVITICUS 11:44

WILL POWER

Do you know of the power
Given to you and me?
Power over all of our problems,
Whatever they may be:
Bills to finances;
What will you will it to be?
Protection for loved ones;
Heartache over broken cars; and lost jobs;
A fix in global situations; to living situations
What will you speak back to our living King?
Marriage?
Divorce.
Which way is it that we will be?
The tongue is mightier than the sword
Now what are you speaking into being?
I bet you can change the planet
If you so speak it be.
Just use your tongue,
And allow your will to be
In alignment with the will of the King.
Watch how it will flow abundantly and plentifully
Like a great tree when we enter into a covenant with He.
No, I can't save the world
But we did save him and them,
Her and us,

She and me.

Until we changed from the way we used to be.

Don't know exactly where it is that we're going

Wheels furiously turning

But moving nowhere!

Feet spinning like cartoon characters

Yet physically we are moving nowhere.

In who is it that we can really move?

From lies to the truth

When in His will is how we really move.

The good is the love in us

When evil is always out to make us do!

Implanted in our traditional ways

From descendants unto our own DNA.

To know God is to live in God

Knowing that She lives in me.

Putting mine own mind away!

Why would dreams not come true

If they've been derived through the King?

Why not to make His own thoughts become real

Through you or through me?

In this world of dreams, his vessels are you and me!

Dear Lord, please use us according to your will.

Correct the stubbornness in your kids!

Allow the spirit to speak straight through our mouths.

Dear Lord,

Show your people what they need to know going froward.

Tell them what they need to hear.

We know that you make us better

And that's why we stay here.

Grasping onto your love.

When His numbers are so few,

The chosen few,

Called unto this Pastor here.

You know that we're listening

All eyes on you when you're ministering.

Minds stayed on your wisdom

We thank Him for sending you to us.

Looking into you I see He

Knowing that you are in God

Knowing that you will help us get to where She needs us to be.

Willing to be like you

Who wants to be like Mike?

Jordan didn't die for ya!

Let's get our minds set on Christ!

Will it to be through love.

Willfully use us Lord,

Allow the self to surrender

Captured in your love.

Coming lowly is us!

Patience, Love, and longsuffering

What will you will it to be?

It may not look like it, but the victors are you and me.

Abundance, plenteousness, and prosperity

Multiplied is what we expect.

From a bad situation unto a good

All through He is what we expect.

Will it to be His life,

In this life,

And watch how He'll put you at your best!

Simply a vessel in a vein,

Transporting a need is thee.

What will you use your willpower for?

Let His power

Flow through you like the sea.

WHAT DOES THE SPIRIT TELL YOU TO DO?

In the morning bright and early
Can you hear the spirit talking to you?
My sheep know My voice and they listen.
Telling you exactly what to do
Yet and still we all confused.
Wanting to go our own way,
Knowing that His way is our best. Still trying to do it our way.
Some say they won't go, yet follow.
Some say they will go and never show
Who knows the final outcome until we get there
And can take the final tally?
What is to be?
My lucky number seven!
And how many times multiplied will you forgive me?
Because I am such a sinner
Still trying to make my way into heaven,
That I must admit.
If love shall cover a multitude of sins
I come to you lowly again.
Knowing that you will fix me again,
How many times will you take me back
Before my guilt becomes too much for me deal with?
How many times do I end up with this feeling?
Just wanting to lie down and let the world take me in?

It is you who carries me, the one who brings me in.
It's already mid-afternoon and inside your voice is all clouded.
Intercepted by the calls of the world
I make my journey from your surroundings.
I stand in you the whole time,
Not knowing that it's you,
Believing that it is me!
When the whole time the ground doesn't even touch my feet,
In the evening,
When I'm so tired,
How could I ever hear your voice?
When the world has knocked me down
And I'm feeling drained, tired, and hoarse.
Not wanting to wake up.
Just to sleep,
And to dream that with you is where I sleep.
Who notices the indwelling spirit
When we face life on our own?
Back to the world
Going down on my own.
That last one!
Was a cold storm to get through,
But I'm ready to do it again!
Just to prove my love to you,
Jesus you are my redeemer and my best friend.

And for my today
Yours was a hefty price to pay.
What does the Spirit tell you?
Now be obedient and do what It's instructing you to do.

........In the night time, when the sun is down,
What does the voice say then?
My sheep know My voice and they hear me.
What is it that you want me to do?
Sleep in a world filled with dreamers?
Dream in a world filled with sleepers?
Pray some more!
In your dark closet get down to your knees,
Even some more!
Never enough of a good thing.
Read the book some more.

My sheep know My voice
Are you listening?

Doing exactly what SHE needs!!

STANDING ON HOLY GROUND

In the Old Testament,
Moses was instructed to remove his shoes.
Thank you Lord Jesus, for giving us this here new.
Stable is the ground that you're standing on
Even when the earth feels shaky beneath you.
Watch as the earth crumbles beneath your feet,
But his Holiness won't allow you to be moved.
Can you see my Jesus, standing amidst those waves?....
Now why can't He, in midair, do the same thang?
We just have to have the faith!
To let Him do things by His name.
By faith, Peter shows us what we will do
When only we believe.
Jesus told him to come.
He didn't begin to sink until he lost sight of his belief.
With his thoughts on the world
Rather than his mind stayed on Christ.
Thought he would sink,
So they had to send out a rescue party to revive him to life!
Jesus won't call you all the way out here,
Just to let you fail!   Peace be still,
And the whole storm passed away!
Whatever it is shall be,
But only according to our faith.
We standing on Holy ground,

Even in the midst of these seemingly rocky sails.
Still fearful for our lives!
When Jesus peacefully sleeps through the night.
Though He's over there stowed away.
Why should our fear make Him rise?
Why wake the chosen one?
All of the work She's been doing, She must be tired;
Let Her sleep!
Yet our fears still cause Her to come and see;
Face all smiles: OH YE OF LITTLE FAITH…..
PEACE BE STILL….

One who can't make up the mind
Is like the waves of the sea!
Tossed about to and fro,
Sounds like one of satan's lines to me.
We must boldly comply
When the Lord says which way we are to be
Making the decision to be bold when God says when and where
He needs us to be.
No time to ask where, when, why or how He wants us gone,
Must just move in what She says
When it's shaky ground that we're standing on.
How many intercessory prayers did it take to save just me? And
How many of his children across the world are in worse shape
Than me?

God has informed you to move
Get out of the way if that's what He needs you to do.
Sometimes it's not until we've been obedient
And lives are changed
Before we can look back and say:
So that is why you moved me to where you needed me to be!
We don't have to understand, when God needs it to be.
We are pre-programmed to hear His voice
Don't let yourself talk yourself out of a great thing.
Go ask for the jars, and fill them with the last of your oil;
Although this menial task may not seem to fit the need.
God doesn't have to explain His story to you or to me.
Did we create Him? Or is it He that created we?
We are only here to be the Lord's servants
No glory is accredited to me.
All the glory and honor must be attributed to our King.
From shaky ground to Holy ground. If that's what you
command It to be!
We can't even understand the earthly realm
Yet of the spiritual we plead.
My God has none of the limitations
That have been placed upon you or on me.
Women to be closer!
Look at all the Matriarchs we leave.
Men we must stand up and be accountable
For the voids that we may leave.

It may look like we're standing on shaky ground,
But I know that it's Holy!
All according to what Jesus said it will be.

UNBREAKABLE

Minister Briscoe!
Your sermon has been on my mind again
Can't shake the thought,
So I asked the Holy Spirit to let creativity chime in again.
From not easily broken
To unbreakable we shall stand.
In how many different ways
Has the world expected that you would just cave in?
To crumble into nothingness
With no help and no one to call
There's only one that we should rely on
And He is always on call.
Maybe not to give the answer
Exactly where and when we may think we need it to be.
He's an on time God,
Who moves with grandeur,
We are His most valued completion.
Some may believe He's too late.
Well is there anything too hard for the Lord?
It's all just to build our faith
These unbelieving children of the world.
There is no promise of tomorrow,
Sometimes it's even difficult to claim for today.
If the Lord wills,
I just want to move out of His way!
Allow the Lord a hostile takeover

Let Him do a raid on this wicked place!
Searching out the heart and mind
Before leaving His stamp across the face.
Once He does,
Know that it's all up to us!
To occupy this space that He has left behind in us.
You know the parable of the spirit who was cast out
And came back seven times again?
Well they were all unclean
And looking for some vacant space to reside in.
What will you do with your mind,
After He clears out your cluttered space?
I am a living testimony,
Just wanting to finish this tiring race.
I should have been dead and gone,
Thank Jesus!
That God let me live on.
What is a testimony without the tests?
We continue to move right on through all this mess.
All the glory be to God
My faith is all in the hope He keeps giving to us.
In alignment with His will
Is the way to bring the most out of us.
Just surrender it to the Lord! Right now
Give it to Him,
And don't quit giving, until there is no more left to give.

Finances, loved ones, circumstances and situations,
Bills and living conditions
To Him don't quit giving.
There's only one thing we can control
And that's the inner we.
Even in stressful times,
Positivity will breed.
Unbreakable is the way
That we stand on our own two feet.
The Lord God gets all of the credit
For allowing us to stand unbreakable,
As his kings and queens.
Nothing in this world can shake us
When we speak life to be.
Speak your life to be unbreakable
And watch what you end up to be.

THEN I WILL CONFESS TO YOU THAT YOUR OWN RIGHT
HAND CAN SAVE YOU

JOB 40:14

ON FIRE

If you were hot I could drink you
If you were cold I could sip you down
But because you are lukewarm I will spit you
Out of my mouth.

If fire is a bad thing
Then why are we burning for the Lord?
The corrupter tries to cool us
Yet we know how to keep these coals aglow.
Poking and prodding until the fire has again grown.
Time can't cover my flame up;
We dance around to keep the flame going.
Reading of the word,
Praying and meditating like never before.
He is the absolute best of me;
Walking and talking
Along these mental coastal shores.
Many times I am able to walk,
And lots of others there's only one pair of footprints on the shore.
While we walk, or He carries me
I spit out all of my cares of this world!
He listens with no defenses,
Just letting me vent till my throat begins to become sore.
Without partiality He guides me
No favoritism thrown my way.

Yes we do have favor in the Lord,
But that's a poetic for another day.
My spirit is on fire!
Soul is aflame!
This fire burns so high one could feel it
From many many miles away.

Come close to my countenance
Let this aroma move your way.
If we are one of the seven churches
Then which one is closest to our way?
Maybe from the good of them all
If God approves, we could create an amazing 8th.
God will move from infinity till beyond,
But our lives will pass away.
Yet we are the hope in tomorrow,
And it is only according to our faith.
We are able to move mountains, and tell storms to pass away.
God has given us the power. Don't let yours wither away.

Mountains thrown into the ocean
Are not as big as they once may have seemed.
The faith to move the whole world
Lies within the thoughts of you and me!
Mental prospects projected, until the growth is highly noticeable.

The low man wins the race, Show my Lord how low you are
Willing to go for Him.
How much energy do you exert, to get down on your knees?
When times are good,
Or when life ain't quite going the way the mind sees.
Whatever the situation may be
To God let's be glad.
Prayer, joy and thanksgiving to be our favorite things we may
Ever have.
This fire burns mightily
Because in God
We are divine beings.
Our souls are on fire
And this mighty energy all flows from She.

BATTLING FOR THE LORD

Find us in a battle with our weaknesses
Just looking to find some strength.
When the whole time
The best thing we could do is to put all our faith into Him.

A cold....The flu,
From cancer to H.I.V.
How could we have financial issues
When it's God that provides for you and me?

Find us polishing our weapons of spiritual warfare
Waiting as the world mounts its attacks.

Reinforcing our shields of salvation,
And adjusting our breastplates of truth for the attack.
Thank God for these boots to get us through
Whatever the filth we must tread through.
The mind of Christ continues to be the light
Allowing our swords to pierce through the night; Exposing truth.
Darkness gives us no fright
Because it is the Lord's word that continues to shine so bright.
Find us locked away in isolation
Searching out the correct way to go.
Good!......Or bad?
Which voice on the shoulder will grow?

When evil just ain't slick enough
Why wouldn't we stick with the good?
On this journey, with the Lord as our Shepherd
We hear the voice as we should.
These solar storms and sun spots
Are only a tip of the iceburg for the uprising of the Lord.
There will be no doubt when the sky shines bright with the Glory
Of our Lord.

The world around us tells us to just give in.
Asking us why do we try?
Why put so much faith in Him?
How could death come back to life?
Speaking only of wars, pestilence, environmental phenoms
And ultimately the end!
Even when Our Father comes
We'll still be on the chase
Reaching out for others that are willing to come home with Him.
No it won't be too late
Find us scrambling through this life
These souls on a mission; Messengers of Christ!
Willing our beings to save souls
And restoring to those what's been taken by might.
Right through the sounds of the trumpet,
Reddening of the seas.
Loathsome sores and men scorched

Through these warnings from the Lord we will continue,
So take heed.
Through death, scarcity, and conflict on earth
We only have hope.
Knowing that we will walk through this valley
Because God is our only hope.
Refusing to let us go,
No matter how deep into the pit He may need us to go.
Not afraid to enter the devil's camp
And take back what's been taken from before.
Thank you for your guidance,
And giving us the courage to follow where you lead.
Showing the Pastor the correct way,
So She continues to successfully show us the way She leads.
So many move aimlessly, confusedly and in a hurry
We use our light to shine on in a dark world
The Lord is never in a hurry!
How much oil have you for your lamp?
Don't get left out in the cold
When the Prince does come back
We must be prepared for what will unfold.
See we battle time, friends, family, material possessions and sin!
Whatever it may be:
Battling to pay bills or find work.
When the whole time we can just give the battle to Him.

MIRACLE WORKER

Who believes in the power, that God has
To do the unthinkable?
Some rely on man,
Others on the government,
But with one backlash of HIS mighty right hand.....
She can cause all these problems to come to an end.
During high unemployment rates, they look to the government for
Jobs.
We get down on our knees and know that
God will provide our jobs.
When The Great Spirit tells you to go fish
Will you stand there and look crazy?
Or will you do what She says, in order to go pay Caesar what is his!
This mindset thinks in another way;
With Christ as the author of it!

Social security provided through faith!
Hands restored by our belief.
Some believe our church mother is gone.
God tells me she's still here with us, sitting right there in her seat.
Health and prosperity be to Mother Cooley and Mother Linda!
How many of us have been turned around? And we know that it's
Only the Lord that could have spent us.
The Lord has provided this family a grant
Thrown to us from a window in heaven.

Just get down on your knees, until the blessing has landed.

The Lord is willing, but only according to our faith.

The faith in the unseen

Is why I walk around with my eyes closed all day;

Moving ahead, only by faith.

The prince of darkness is the master of deception.

Our Father will never speak in lies, His words are our blessings!

Miracle mom still here!

Though evil forces attempted to take her life.

I stand here to speak the Lord's Word

For at least one more time!

The children in the Kingdom hall

Represent the longevity of this church's life!

By faith, I claim to be the first soul to get dunked

When next door is an open space for revival.

To only envision the finished product!

When unbelievers could never imagine from the broken space.

Just can't fathom the potential in our reason for such a high faith.

So many scared of success, or failure, so they figure why try.

How can we die when in reality, we've never even really tried?

The miracle of life is all in our ability to live.

Our mother in here elderly, with the heart of a kid.

Call me one of the prophets in Acts,

I'm just bragging on what She's did!

Pulled us together

Different faces, races, and beliefs! Adults and kids;

Here is the place we need to be.

I never would have known any of yall
If God didn't want this union to live!
By faith we intercede, while down here on our knees.
Thank you for putting this music in our heart
And granting us this ability to sing.
Know that he who searches out his Kingdom
All else shall follow with ease!
Just taking some time out to count our blessings
And recap on these things done for us by Our Father;
Our King!

TRAVELING THIS ROAD

Who is it that I may see as I journey?
Will I notice you right here walking next to me?
Moving from here to over there
Hoping for the conversion to bring about change within me.
What is it that may change me?
Such the sinner that my mind would see.
Turning this life around!
Once the time comes that I'm touched by His being;
Like Lazarus, I have become unbound.
Only to touch the hem is all that my mind's eye can see.
How is it that I know that evil won't bring me back down?
And how many times must you come back for me?
Until I am finally lifted up forevermore,
Standing tall with the King?
Most people still see me as I used to be
Well that spirit has no more life in me.
From Saul to Paul,
Abram to Abraham,
Jeremiah was called as a youth.
Walking the road to fix the city of a stiff necked generation.
Peter is known as a rock.
What's exactly in a name?
The label that was given to me,
The one before this conversion began.
What will you now call me? Knowing that I am a changed man.

This road is not exactly where I planned to be,
Not even tired yet, of that there ol' man.
Now here I find myself, on this road to change,
From what it is that I was, long before this conversion began.
To what it is that God needs me to be.
The spirit had to force change!
How much force is needed to transform me
From who I was, to what it is that my vision
Just could not yet see.
Not looking for any yellow bricks
Just hoping to take the right path at this here fork in the road.
Simply to sit down for some seconds and meditate
Asking God which way is the best way for me to go?
How long am I to wait
Before the Holy Spirit comes to let me know?
My patience is what I ask you to work on
And with this my anxiousness only seems to grow all the more.
Nobody said the road was to be easy,
And most times I feel so all alone.
I came to find out, that it is sometimes when I feel so alone,
That I know I'm going the way that I'm supposed to go.
Conversing with my thoughts,
Listening to what you communicate to me.
I'll just keep traveling this road
Until you lead me exactly where it is
That you want me to be.

THE SIGN OF A VICTORY

Pre-told in a legacy, some refuse to believe.
Written down for this world,
But understanding only comes to those who read.
With wisdom as my sister, and understanding as my next of kin
How could evil ever expect to beat me?
How could the corrupter ever expect to win?
Trip me when you can
You love to see me fall down,
But the Spirit of the Lord will pick me right back up
You could never rob my Queen of Her crown.
No way you can rob She of this victory
There's only One who descended to ascend.
Making a way for those of us who are still down here;
A way for us to get back up there.
In glory with Him.

What is the sign that lets me know
That God has opened up the door?
Is it the rainbows in the sky?
Could it be the Doves flying high?
What about the fleece that lies in the morning dew,
Yet remains dry?
Is it this picture in my pocket
That keeps my mind stayed on you?
That's the sign of a victory, and the story aint even yet through.
My latter days will be my better days
That is what was already promised through you.

50

Like a king on his throne,

You put me here and can just as easily pull us on through.

Your love provides the strength

For us to move on for just one more day.

See me wrestling with your spirit, until my joint slips out of place.

Furthering me to walk with a dip for life

While traveling down this road!

Must I persecute you?

Then here! Just take away my life!

It's yours anyway; I hand it back, on a silver plate.

It's all about you Lord,

My thoughts don't matter anyway.

With the mind stayed on Jesus

Why would evil ever dare to challenge us anyway?

Fasting until my vision is blurred,

And my heart starts to beat out of place.

No. Not afraid of death!

Because it is the Lord that lives in us.

You meant for this to hurt me,

But God gave this to good.

What the Lord has in store?

The sign of a victory;

The strength to keep us moving forward!

Pushing the way through this dark forest.

WITH MEN IT IS IMPOSSIBLE, BUT NOT WITH GOD; FOR
WITH GOD ALL THINGS ARE POSSIBLE.

MARK 10:27

WE ON A WAR PATH

The enemy surrounds us, expecting us to break down.

We are outnumbered and outgunned yet we refuse to back down.

Ammunition running short, but faith won't let us quit.

Persecuted for our beliefs,

Yet we know God is in the midst of this.

Accuracy is of keen importance

Not a shot to waste. No we can't miss.

Ready......Steady.......Aim.......

Now that's a direct hit.

Right between the eyes!

Just one more for the home team.

Have you ever seen the movie 300?

We'll there's 3,000 against just me!

Calm and cool to be our countenance

Because we train for this.

On every Tuesday, Friday, Saturday and Sunday

I said we train for this:

From Matthew to Mark. Acts to Ephesians;

The Old Testament or the new,

Our general leads us well in this.

She's been ordained for leading these troops!

Simply exercising our thoughts for truth.

The head is where the war is won

And the battlefield is in the mind.....

How fitted is your helmet that you have on for this?

How will you protect your mind?

54

Coming at us in seven ways but the enemy flees in 49.
This warfare is spiritual,
And it's been going since the beginning of time.
This war has nothing to do with me
We give this life to Christ.
Dominating this battlefield
With the power given by the Governor of life!
The just shall live by faith.
With the Lord as our shepherd
How could we ever get bound in time?
We've been given this power!
So don't be afraid to use your mind.
The enemy will mount up against us,
But it's his own soldiers that will be taken away.
Attracted to our side, stepping into the bright light.
Coming out of the darkness and gloominess,
Just wanting to do what's right.
Until the minority becomes the majority
And the few becomes the new!
We continue to keep on battling
Through this valley of darkness we must tread through.
Not afraid of these dark surroundings
It's for our Lord that we are down
Here to convert these lost souls
Before reclaiming our crowns!
In my Father's house there are many mansions
This world will come to an end.

Yet the Father's love will never die
Keeps on growing from everlasting to everlasting.
Those warriors can't scare us
We know that we are born to win.
Like terrorists on a mission
We're ready and willing to lose our lives for Him!
Yeah, we done lost our minds, and we ain't trying to find em!
Christ has given us this new mind,
It's all for His glory, and we standing right here behind Him.
Blinded by the light,
Makes it hard to see
So we just close our eyes
Knowing that it's the Holy Spirit that takes the lead.
Looking around this battlefield. It's only us left!
All those who came to attack us
Now lie on the battlefield dead.
Waiting for My Lord to come
And resurrect the life.
We stand on this battlefield victorious,
Gloriously screaming: All glory be to Christ!
Who would have believed we could do this?
The power of God has won.
We will never stop fighting
This war has only just begun.

EVEN OUR CHANGE HAS PURPOSE

Pennies, nickels, dimes, quarters, half dollar or dollar pieces!
Whatever it may be; we collecting all these pieces.
Having all faith in the magic these will bring.
Lord willing, we can take one penny and double it
Every day by faith.
Compound to be our interest;
In only 30 days. We'll have more than enough to give away
In accordance to our faith. This change gon' come, even if not today.
Growing exponentially,
Until our days are done.
All for Gods purpose, we will put to use these funds.
Let's continue to fill baby food jars,
Or improvise and bring whatever;
Feel free to fill up mason jars. If in those, the blessing can be savored.
This is the time of year that we plant seed
For the June harvest to come.
June boasts a harvest of no planting
Excitedly anticipating the autumn harvest to come.
Isaac went forth under the Lords instructions;
Then Isaac sowed in that land and received!
In the same year an hundredfold blessing,
Much more than was the need.
Open up the book to Genesis 26:12
And dare to claim his same blessing.
What kind of situations and circumstances may God allow

In order to bring about HIS blessing.
Will he break me all the way down
Using a new form of Currency?
Even financially, we're not the same people that we used to be
Willing to give our last dollar! If it's employed for the king.
We're earning higher wages
By moving in line to the will of His needs.
Give it all to the Lord!
He's promised His all for us to see.
Never would have made it......If He took His love from our beings.
Trying to do it my way always ended up in disgust.
We plant the seeds,
Titus waters them
But it's only the Lord who knows what plants will come.
Anger, frustration, disappointment and heartache.
Fear and temptation, indecisiveness all must fade away.
Joy, peace, longsuffering He's brought to me
Kindness, goodness and faithfulness to your last day.
He throws these blessings down,
But they only land upon those who are looking to make a play.
Put your hands up and tell the Lord:
Yes! I receive this today.
Tearing down these strongholds, whatever they may be
Even our change has purpose
It is God that attracts this wealth unto me.

Never afraid for our incomes

It's always abundant in the economy of the King

We must be thankful for every blessing

Celebrate even a penny found on the street.

People look at me funny, yet I can only smile.

Weird looks no longer even bother me.

I know that these steps are not mine.

The Lord's way is the only; the worldly shall pass away in time.

See the Lord's blessing for billions of dollars

As it filters right from our minds.

Just a blessing to us.

To be given away.

How to improve the lives of our fellow man for today?

What God gives is abundance.

What can he do with a clenched hand and face?

Open up those palms,

And see what purpose falls into your open space.

HOMECOMING

Don't cry for me during this celebration.
Know that I'm coming home!
I can see all those over there who've come for me,
Waving me along.
Through that opened door!
How could this life ever be over?
Know that it's just the beginning for me
For one more day, we continue to press forward.
In the Lord's house meditating
To those who've already gone this way!
My humbled spirit will remain
To be nutrition to this deficient world for yet another day.
Good seeds planted, in this fertile soil to blossom.
Watch as our tears provide the necessary reign
For Gods garden.
What if I never tried, and just let it all cave in?
Would I still have such a huge showing
From my family, loved ones and friends?
To the end, you all know me to be a soldier for my Lord
Fighting on this battlefield
Until I'm back home with my Lord.
Sitting at Her table,
These steps that we take are Hers.
Jesus came down to get me
With loved ones surrounding him
Welcoming me in!

Many of you may be crying!

Well see the big smile across my face in this picture here?

No time for dying

Only life resides in here.

In life, me and the devil been in a race,

And I must have won, because I'm the first one to make it to this

Beautiful place.

The victory is Hers,

So for this homecoming I will you to dance, sing and shout.

Celebrate until the rising of the morning Son

The ole evil one gets no victory in this house.

Have no doubt!

Just one more testimony,

For God through faith.

I came here to bring life

Doing all of this work by faith.

United in Fearless Faith, just a sojourner in an unfamiliar place.

An alien am I no more.

I dwell amongst the King

So rest assured that even satan couldn't stop me from reaching

Our Heavenly Fathers kingdom.

If death is the mother of beauty then what level of beauty do you

See when you look at me?

Can you see me up here waving!

Wings soaring out behind me.

Many may ask why,
But it's not up to you, or I.
I have to go!
All about my Father's business
Is all that I can tell you for why.

The hope in the rainbows should clear those
Tear drops from your eyes!
My God does not believe in death
He is the Governor of Life.

WE LOVE YOU MOTHER HOWELL!!

TREADING THROUGH THIS STORM

From this destination to the next won
I know that I'm safe in your arms;
Comfortably nestled!
Flying high amongst your stars.
I am the recipient of this
Because I reach out to receive it.
Arms spread wide to your goodness
Enjoying this feeling of great peacefulness.
The wind blows mightily,
Pushing the word through my stumbling heart.
Feeble and weak, my knees shake to your goodness,
Your love deep within my heart.
I am the last one left
His kingdom resides within me.
Through the mighty wind storms and artic temps
To the finish line we must proceed.
Not to the biggest, nor to the strongest, but to His.
When the cold storms resemble hailstorms
Will we be able to let bygones be bygones?
This is the way to get us back to Him.
Instead you seek the way out of the storm.
Slipknotted into this twisted game
Of western world street fame.
Projected onto a wall of illusion.
Not knowing exactly what it is that we were planned to be.
Fighting to make the way back to Him.

Drifting amongst the forceful world;
Not believing in the power of He.
I can change the course of the world......
Now you say it back to me.
What is the level of excellence we demand?
When we just dare to trust and believe.
Continue fighting through this cold storm or barren trees.
Even when the bone chilling winds push us back,
Tired and weak!
Cold and hungry, still we fight back.
We continue to run the race
So glad to get through this way.
I gracefully look forward to each and every new day.
When the world tells me I can't
I battle forward any way.
Thank you Minister Briscoe
For informing me to repeat the Lord's name.
Jesus is my hero
Without Him how could we be saved?
I am but a sinner
Yet and still He knows my name.
Communicating with me personally, as He leads the way
Dropped off at the House of the King
For those who dare to follow
The ones not scared away.
The way He leads looks impossible,

but only with men,

and those who dont have power by refusing to believe in Him.

I practice the power of God

And through SHE we will do anything.

Even though this road looks rough

I would never trade it in.

Believe through all faith in Jesus

That He knows the way to bring us in.

THE KING IS HERE

Thank you for your Holy Spirit,
I can feel your presence in me.
You are always here with me
Even when I can't physically feel you near to me.
Knowing that when I can't walk
It is you who carries me.
Found me crying, down on my knees, and you still wouldn't
Let the world bury Me.
Just picked me up, and wiped me clean,
When I wanted to stay down on the ground
For the world to just put an end to my being.
When the world continued to kick,
Suggesting for me to just stay down.
It was the whisper in my ear, of your ever-present voice
Advising me not to give up and reminding me to stay tough.
To put myself aside and only think of your cause
No matter what the world may say
We know this place is not of us.
Heavenly and Holy
I continue to read your scriptures.
Eyes battered and bruised,
Yet I keep on reading.
Lips bleeding and swollen,
Yet I continue believing.
Talking to myself repeating: JUST TO GET OUT OF THE WAY.

Let the Lord do His work,
In His own way.
Please take this cup of suffering away from me...
I hope you can finish that phrase.
To be close to the King
Sometimes is to be so far away.
My Father wasn't always around
Yet I still turned out O.K.
An anomaly to the stereotypes,
From trouble I turned away.
My city still managed to call me back
When from it I ran away.
Landed in the belly of the fish,
Anticipating the release date.
Watching as my world falls
Caves in all around this space.
When it is that I am weak
The King in me is abound.
Giving my all away
Trusting that God keeps me from falling down.
The King is here,
And SHE and HE are won.

MY GRACE IS SUFFICIENT FOR YOU, FOR MY STRENGTH IS
MADE PERFECT IN WEAKNESS.

2 CORINTHIANS 12:9

www.ingramcontent.com/pod-product-compliance
Lightning Source LLC
Chambersburg PA
CBHW021213020426
42331CB00003B/336